Trust Rules!

TRUST BASED SUCCESS

Proven Ways to
Stop Stressing and
Start Living

MARK GIVEN
Founder of the Trust Based Philosophy™

Copyright © 2018 Mark Given

ALL RIGHT RESERVED. No part of this book or its associated ancillary materials may be reproduced or transmitted in any form or by any means, electronic or mechanical, including photocopying, recording, or by any informational storage or retrieval system without permission from the publisher.

For publishing consideration:
markgivenseminars@gmail.com

ISBN: 978-1-7320146-2-6

DISCLAIMER AND/OR LEGAL NOTICES

While all attempts have been made to verify information provided in this book and its ancillary materials, neither the author nor publisher assumes any responsibility for errors, inaccuracies or omissions and is not responsible for any financial loss by customers in any manners. Any slights of people or organizations are unintentional. If advice concerning legal, financial, accounting or related matters in needed, the services of a qualified professional should be sought. This book and its associated ancillary materials, including verbal and written training, in not intended for use as a source of legal, financial or accounting advice. You should be aware of the various laws governing business transactions or other business practices in your particular geographic location.

The author has made every effort to ensure the accuracy of the information within this book was correct at time of publication. The author does not assume and hereby disclaims any liability to any party for any loss, damage, or disruption caused by errors or omissions, whether such errors or omissions result from accident, negligence, or any other cause.

Any examples, stories, references or case studies are for illustrative purposes only and should not be interpreted as testimonies and/or examples of what reader and/or consumers can expect. Any statements, strategies, concepts, techniques, exercises and ideas in this information, materials and/or seminar training offered are simply opinion or experience, and thus should not be misinterpreted as promises.

WHAT OTHERS ARE SAYING...

"Having known Mark Given for 20 years, I know he lives his philosophy of *TRUST* Based Leadership, Sales and Success every day. He has shared that knowledge with you in this book."

    Zan Monroe, CEO, Author, Speaker and Coach

"There are writers and speakers and then there are teachers. My good friend Mark is a teacher. He has captured the essence of the most critical aspect of relationships in a way that made me reflect on my own life and leadership. This short read has long-term impact. Thank you Mark for compiling such profound information on a *Trust Based Philosophy*."

    Jackie Leavenworth, Author, International Speaker, Trainer and Business Coach

"My friend, Mark Given has created his life and business based on building *Trust*. Now you have an amazing opportunity to learn his Trust Based Philosophy. Read his book.....it can change your life!"

    Jo Mangum, Coach, Trainer, Author of *The Strategic Agent*®

"Mark lives his life by the values he shares about *Trust*. This book will not only show you how to build *Trust*, but how to use it and apply the principles in your everyday life. This book is a must read!"

    Lee Barrett, Author, Tutor, National Real Estate Instructor, Broker

"I've not only had the privilege of seeing Mark teach but also taught alongside him so I know firsthand that as a teacher and author his message is engaging ... genuine ... and, impactful! If you have not yet had the "Mark experience" this is a must read."

Ed Hatch, International NLP Speaker, Author, Coach, Negotiation Expert

"Having worked with Mark in business and volunteer situations, he has my complete *Trust*. His books share discoveries and techniques that are easy to understand and implement immediately."

Pat Zaby, REALTOR® and Highly Respected National Speaker and Teacher

"*Trust* Mark to create strategies that can be immediately implemented by everyone!"

Frank Serio, Past National President Council of Residential Specialists

"Mark has provided for us an excellent resource to apply what we know is needful for *Trust*. I love his list of concepts to make ourselves more trustworthy. The beauty in this book is in asking yourself the questions he provides and adding thoughtful answers to lock the concept into your regular practice of leading."

Monica Neubauer, Speaker, Podcaster

"Mark is a Master Teacher and his Trust Based Philosophy has the power to improve lives and businesses."

Larry Kendall, Author of Ninja Selling

Speaking Testimonials

"If you are looking for a speaker, trainer and coach that can empower, inspire, and motivate your group then you must book my friend Mark Given!"

James Malinchak, Featured on ABC's *Secret Millionaire*, Best Selling Author of 20 Books

"We hire Mark to share his Trust Based Philosophy in leadership, sales and success with our 1500 members every year!"

Zan Monroe, CEO Long Leaf Pine Association, Author, Speaker and Coach

"You are simply an event planners dream! I have been involved with contracting hundred's of speakers for various programs over the last 24+ years and I consider Mark as an exemplary example of an ideal speaker."

Rebecca Fletcher, Director, GIRE – VP of Education

"My reason for inviting you back time and time again is purely selfish…it makes me look good. I thank you for the time you invest in crafting your message to meet our specific needs. I thank you for the energy you pump into our company. And, I thank you for your friendship. You are a class act that is very good at what you do. I look forward to our continued relationship and am anxious to have you back soon!"

Kit Hale, Principal Broker / Managing Partner MKB, REALTORS

DEDICATION

It is with profound admiration, respect and love that I dedicate this book and all that I do personally and professionally to my wonderful wife Janice, our sons Blaine, Chase, Kyle, Taylor, our daughter Kerri, our daughters-in-law Janelle, Bonnie, Lauren, and Gabbie and our son-in law Dylan, as well as our growing crop of beautiful and gifted grandchildren. Without them, my life and work would be incomplete and I would not know the joy I have experienced nearly every day of my life. Through the years, I have learned and grown because of many master teachers and speakers that have inspired me. Some know who they are and some don't, but none the less, I thank each of you. Most recently, I have reached new levels of professional growth because of my coach and friend James Malinchak. James....... you ROCK! And, without reservation, I thank my Heavenly Father and his Son, of which I believe, none of the positive I have experienced in my life would have been possible and they have proven over and over that there is nearly nothing impossible with focus followed by ACTION!

Building greater **Trust** begins now...

"People begin to become SUCCESSFUL the minute they decide to be!"

CONTENTS

Proven Way #1
Time Wasted is Time Forever Lost –
The Problem with Television 13

Proven Way #2
Time Wasted is Time Forever Lost –
The Problem with Social Media 16

Proven Way #3
Time Wasted Is Time Forever Lost –
The Problem with Interruptions 20

Proven Way #4
Principles of Time Management 23

Proven Way #5
Seven HUGE Questions 28

Proven Way #6
SUCCESS Begins With FOCUS 30

Proven Way #7
Your Personal Habits 34

Proven Way #8
10 Amish Business SUCCESS Strategies 37

Proven Way #9
SUCCESSFUL People Have a Winning Mindset 40

Proven Way #10
Deep Knowledge VS. Deep Skills 44

Proven Way #11
9.5 ACTION Steps to Improving YOUR Life 48

Proven Way #12
The Beauty in Signature Strengths 52

Proven Way #13
13 Points to Creating YOUR Successful Life 56

Proven Way #14
"Just a Little" Might Be the Right Amount...................... 59

Proven Way #15
Practice Makes Better... 62

Proven Way # 16
Bad Things Happen to Good People............................ 66

Proven Way #17
Success Leaves Clues.. 69

Proven Way #18
Systems Keep You from Going Insane......................... 74

Proven Way #19
Working On vs. Working In Your Life 78

Proven Way #20
Change Your Mind...Change Your Life 82

Proven Way #21
Suck It Up!.. 85

Proven Way #22
It's Now How YOU Wow!.. 90

Proven Way #23
How's YOUR Funny Bone... 93

Proven Way #24
When You Need Something...Ask................................. 96

Proven Way #25
4 Steps to Succeeding at Anything 100

One Last Message from Mark 105

Book Bonus
10 <u>More</u> Well Known Secrets of Southern Hospitality...109

Additional Book Bonus
Mark Given Interviewed by Jack Canfield 113

Proven Ways to Create YOUR Trust Based SUCCESS Philosophy Start NOW... so let's get rolling!!

TRUST BASED SUCCESS

A TRUST BASED PHILOSOPHY

MARK GIVEN

A MESSAGE TO YOU FROM MARK!

I am Mark Given, an enthusiastic motivational speaker, teacher and Amazon #1 Bestselling Author. I have written several self improvement books and have spoken at more than 1000 programs across this planet. You may not know me from my books or seminars, but one thing you should know is that we are both very much alike.

Every day, *just like you*, I strive to be my best and focus on making a positive difference in this wonderful world.

You want to SUCCEED, help your family, be a good friend, make a secure living and be remembered as someone that can be *trusted*. Me too!

You already know that building or rebuilding **Trust** is a top priority for companies looking to sell more products, serve more people and capture their markets.

Trust is a critical link to all good relationships whether personal or professional.

Trust is a primary factor in how people work together effectively, build powerful relationships and listen to one another.

Lack of **Trust** creates poor productivity and low energy.

So, in this important book, you'll learn how to build **Trust** in many ways and do it more often.

You'll learn how to lead by example, communicate more openly, take responsible action and create more personal **SUCCESS**.

Read this book then share it with a friend. They **Trust** your opinion.

And, thank-you for taking the time to INVEST IN YOURSELF AND IN YOUR FUTURE!

PROVEN WAY #1

TIME WASTED IS TIME FOREVER LOST—THE PROBLEM WITH TELEVISION

What would have to happen in the next 3 years for you to feel happy with your SUCCESS or progress?

Don't play this card to lightly. The next 3 years are going to come and go as quickly as the blink of an eye. Don't think so… just ask your mother.

So, if you are reading this book to become more SUCCESSFUL, then what is your biggest time suck?

If you're like most people, those time sucks would be TV, social media and interruptions.

I'll address each one separately since improving in each area is so very important to creating your most SUCCESSFUL life.

I read a study recently that showed;

The average American 12 and older spends 1,704 hours watching television every year

That's 4.7 hours on average with a TV on every day

That's almost 33 hours every week—more than a full day distracting their mind and filling their brain with what Hollywood believes they need to know.

That's the equivalent of watching television for two solid months every year. No wonder we're struggling to maintain a highly intelligent society and we're falling behind many other countries of the world.

What's the solution?

- 30 minutes of reading every day x 5 days every week = *150 min*
- 150 minutes x 50 weeks = *7500 min of reading*
- 7500 minutes ÷ 60 min = *125 hrs of reading every year*

That's the equivalent of five full days of reading each and every year.

If you took my advice and added 5 full days of reading to your life every year, don't you think you'd learn some incredible things?

You shouldn't cheat by just reading novels or People Magazine either.

Read trade magazines, blogs, self-help and motivational books.

Stay away from internet news and gossip articles.

In only 30 minutes spread out through the course of your day, this one simple act would improve your mind and increase your depth of knowledge.

Ten minutes when you wake up, five minutes while on a rest break, fifteen minutes during lunch and so many other ways you could make it happen!

Get to work…make the change today…it's only your increased SUCCESS at stake!

> **"The mind, once stretched by a new idea, never returns to its original dimensions."**
> —*Ralph Waldo Emerson*

What would have to happen in the next 3 years for you to feel happy with your SUCCESS or progress?

PROVEN WAY #2

TIME WASTED IS TIME FOREVER LOST—THE PROBLEM WITH SOCIAL MEDIA

A California State University study in 2012 showed that the average college student could go no longer than **four minutes** without texting or consulting social media.

We're not getting better though, we're getting worse.

A recent study by Microsoft showed that a goldfish has a longer attention span than an adult human!

Back in the early 2000's, Tom Peters, a brilliant writer, business thinker and speaker wrote;

"Email is the modern opium of the people"

Today, that has changed. I would say that;

"Social Media is now the modern opium of the people" and YOU might just be one of the millions that are addicted.

According to the Huffington Post, the amount of time people spend on social media has increased steadily over the past several years with teens now spending up to nine hours a day on social platforms. Huffington also noted that 30% of all time spent online is allocated to social media interaction and the average person in America now spends significantly more time in online interactions than in personal interactions. And it's probably no surprise that the majority of time now spent online is on a mobile device (60%).

So, what to do?

You already know that Social Media time isn't all bad.

At times, you've used it wisely and prudently, and when you do, Social Media is a vital tool to SUCCESS.

The magic in your social media tool becomes apparent when you create a system you believe in and will stick to.

My wise friend Rich Sands developed a 10/1/2/3/5 system for Facebook that he says IS magical.

    10 minutes a day

    1 update

    2 new friends

    3 comments

    5 times a week

That's it. Rich says simplicity with Facebook really works and his system can work for anyone.

According to Joel Comm and his book *Twitter Power—How to Dominate Your Market One Tweet at a Time*, the typical Twitter user is age 35—44, but we also can't ignore a majority of users who are high earners and older professionals.

Joel's experience suggests that anyone who uses social media successfully doesn't just create content to post but they also create intentional conversations and those conversations create communities.

You might try it, but use it wisely. Think very clearly before you post. Don't be one of the foolish that burned bridges, ended relationships and lost their future over a stupid and poorly timed tweet. It's amazing how many careers have been lost to 140 characters.

So…what about Instagram, Pinterest and on and on and on.

Eventually, it will all be replaced.

The key to SUCCESS with social media comes from determining what can work best for you, establishing a system that you can live with and then stick to the plan.

> **"Social media is like a drug…
> immediately gratifying and
> hugely addictive!"**
> —*Mark Given*

If you could pick the best 15 — 30 minutes a day to utilize and maximize your social media activities, when would that be and how would you most effectively use that time?

PROVEN WAY #3

TIME WASTED IS TIME FOREVER LOST—THE PROBLEM WITH INTERRUPTIONS

According to Claessens of Technische Universiteit Eindhoven in the Netherlands, we each experience 96 minutes of interruptions every day.

Their study of employees at a multinational company found that on average; just *73%* of planned tasks were completed by the end of the work day.

58% of those employees in the study cited *interruptions* as the reason for leaving tasks incomplete, with the most often occurring *interruption* being colleagues asking questions.

As in many other studies, less-important tasks are somewhat more likely to be completed than more-important tasks.

Does that sound familiar?

In 2013, Gary Keller and Jay Papasan released their book *The One Thing—The Surprisingly Simple Truth Behind Extraordinary Results*. Their research shows that workers are interrupted every 11 minutes and then spend almost one third of their day recovering from all the distractions.

So…How do you solve the problem?

Start with finding somewhere you can work that takes you out of the path of disruption and interruption. Have all your supplies on hand so you don't leave that sacred place except for bathroom breaks. And, turn off your phone, shut down your email, exit your browser and focus on your work for several hours at least 3 times a week.

If you really want to get things done, do it 5 days a week until the project is finished. Try it and you'll be amazed at how much you accomplish!

> **"People who say something is impossible should not interrupt those who are busy getting it done!"**
> *—Mark Given*

Where could you go for solitude that would help you get things done 2 or 3 hours a day 3 to 5 days a week?

_____

_____

_____

_____

_____

_____

_____

_____

_____

_____

_____

_____

_____

_____

_____

_____

_____

_____

_____

_____

PROVEN WAY #4
PRINCIPLES OF TIME MANAGEMENT

Sometimes, as I travel the world speaking and teaching, I begin a program by asking this compelling question;

"Your life or your business would likely improve over the next 12 months if you could learn how too _____"?

The most common answer....Manage Time Better.

Why do I ask that question? Because people everywhere struggle with time management and YOU likely do too.

Here are some facts;

- We all have the same amount of time—1440 minutes every day and 168 hours every week. That's it, no more and no less.

- If we're lucky, we'll have 60 really productive years (I hope I'm wrong about that as it relates to YOU, but for most people, those years begin when we graduate from high school and end somewhere around 80).

What's interesting though is how a few people get an amazing amount done in that period of time while many of the rest of us are running around like chickens with our heads cut off.

So, how do the really SUCCESSFUL few do it?

Time Management.

Many scholars have tackled this problem for centuries.

Pareto studied it in a round-about way. Parkinson and Covey are just a couple of the other notable names that worked on this issue.

Although Pareto wasn't actually studying time management, his conclusion that 80% of your SUCCESS will come from 20% of your tasks is applicable to many things including time.

Parkinson reported that work expands so as to fill the time available for its completion. (In other words, no matter how much time you have to complete a task, the average person will stretch out the task the entire time allotted). Procrastinators, please stand!

Covey broke his study down into 4 quadrants.

Urgent and Important

Not Urgent but Important

Urgent but Not Important

Not Urgent and Not Important

Covey concluded that Quadrant 2—the Not Urgent but Important area is the most critical part of time management and if you read his book *The 7 Habits of Highly Effective People*, it will make sense.

When you ignore important tasks (things like relationships, customers, projects and events), disasters quickly appear and YOU become the one running around like that disembodied chicken, trying desperately to repair the inevitable problems that will arise.

So, going back to my question;

"Your life or your business would most likely improve in the next 12 months if you learned _____"?

What's the solution?

Some time back, Harvard Business Review posted a short article on "5 Things **Super Successful People** do before 8am."

Here are their results:

1. Exercise
2. Visualization
3. Map out the day
4. Eat a healthy breakfast
5. Do the least desirable thing first

Interesting isn't it and you can see that super success isn't always defined as making money, but rather about balance, harmony and focus.

So, if you're already on track and time management isn't an issue for you, or your systems are in place and you are already Super Successful, then pay no attention to Harvard's five principles.

But, if you're struggling with time management and it's keeping you from the SUCCESS you desire………tomorrow morning would be a great day to begin.

And no matter how good you think you are at it, you need to keep making time management a priority or you'll slip back with the rest of us!

> **"Being busy does not always mean real work. The object of all work is production or accomplishment and to either of these ends there must be forethought, system, planning, intelligence, and honest purpose, as well as perspiration. Seeming to do is not doing."**
> *—Thomas Edison*

What _one thing_ could I implement tomorrow morning that would help me reach my definition of Super Successful quicker?

Time management is good in theory, but who has time to get really good at it?

PROVEN WAY #5
SEVEN HUGE QUESTIONS

There are many important questions sprinkled throughout our life that we will struggle with, but as it relates to our mortal SUCCESS, I believe these are the big seven.

1. Who do I want to be?
2. What do I want to do?
3. Where do I want to go?
4. How much is enough?
5. When will I slow down or retire?
6. What will it take to make all this happen?
7. Who can help me SUCCEED and help me fill my life with JOY?

It's only when you get really clear on all these 7 questions that you will create the life you are seeking.

In business, it's done through systems and processes and by writing and clarifying your mission and vision.

In life, you experience ongoing joyful moments through an understanding of what really matters most to YOU, then not letting the thousands of other trivial matters distract you from what's most important.

Take some time this week to consider the answers to these questions. If you do, you'll experience more of the joy you deserve.

> "An important part of finding SUCCESS is preparation on purpose."
>
> —*Mark Given*

Which one of the 7 important questions do I need to be more clear on and when will I begin making a change?

PROVEN WAY #6
SUCCESS BEGINS WITH FOCUS

Some years ago, Chicken Soup for the Soul co-authors Jack Canfield and Mark Victor Hansen, along with Les Hewitt wrote a wonderful book entitled *The Power of Focus—How to Hit Your Personal and Financial Targets with Absolute Certainty.*

In their book, you will find these wise principles;

1. The three biggest challenges facing business people today are: time pressures, financial pressures, and the struggle to maintain a healthy balance between work and home.

2. 90% of people that attend short term seminars see no improvement in their lives because they don't take the time to implement what they learn.

3. The main reason most people struggle professionally and personally is simply a lack of focus.

Pretty smart counsel isn't it?

Life never completely closes the door on opportunity.

When you focus most of your time and energy doing things you are truly brilliant at, you eventually reap big rewards.

I've also learned through many other books, blogs, podcasts and recordings that;

    a. The average person loses focus every 6 to 10 seconds.

b. It's when you focus on creating value in the world around you, for the people around you, that the greatest opportunities will come to you. And they'll come in moments and from places you never expected.

c. There are times in our lives when imbalance <u>is</u> balance, when a short term focus contributes to our overall mission in life.

According to research by Harvard University, only 1 out of every 110 people focus on the way things <u>can be done</u>, the other 109 focus on how they <u>can't be done.</u>

By focusing too much energy on only one thing (the problem), you will likely miss something else vital (the solution).

Harvard said that Extraordinary Results are directly determined by how narrow you can make your focus.

So, with that said, a very important key to your SUCCESS or anyone else's SUCCESS is focus.

How are you making focus your focus?

"Concentrate all your thoughts upon the work at hand. The sun's rays do not burn until brought to a focus."
—*Alexander G. Bell*

Of all the things that I need to focus on right now, what is the one thing that is most important?

Today, our lesson is about goals and targets...
Let's begin with obvious targets that present real opportunity!

PROVEN WAY #7
YOUR PERSONAL HABITS

It's not unusual for people to ask me about books I would recommend, so here's a good one...*The Power of Habit—Why We Do What We Do in Life and Business* by Charles Duhigg.

Charles is just one of many experts on habit changing, and here's what he has to teach us;

- Most of the choices we make each day may feel like the products of **well-considered decision making** but they're not.
- More than **40%** of the actions people perform each day aren't actual decisions at all, **but habits.**
- Your brain can't tell the difference between a *bad habit* and *a good habit*, that's why it's so hard to change.
- Find a simple and obvious cue (the "why") and you can create the habits necessary for SUCCESS.
- When a habit emerges, our brain stops working so hard, so unless you deliberately find new routines, the pattern will not unfold automatically.
- A habit cannot be eradicated, it must instead be replaced.
- If you want to change a habit, you must find an alternative routine, and your odds of SUCCESS go up dramatically when you commit to changing your habit as part of a group or community.
- A company with dysfunctional habits can't turn around simply because a leader orders it.

- If you believe you can change, and you are willing to do what's necessary to change, the change then becomes real and your brain embraces the new habit.

I've left out a depth of detail and research, and Charles gives you a formula to make habit changing possible, so go get the book or listen to it in an audio file. It could be life changing for you!

If you're interested in other books that can help you change your bad habits, these would be good choices for you as well:

- Keys to SUCCESS—Napoleon Hill
- The Monk Who Sold His Ferrari—Robin Sharma
- The SUCCESS Principles—Jack Canfield
- The Answer—John Assaraf

> **"Champions don't do extraordinary things. They do ordinary things, but they do them without thinking, too fast for the competition to react. They follow the habits they've learned."**
> *—Tony Dungy*

If there is one habit I need to break today, what is it?
If there is one habit I need to gain today, what is it?

PROVEN WAY #8
10 AMISH BUSINESS SUCCESS STRATEGIES

You will likely never read the book *Success Made Simple—an inside look at why Amish businesses thrive* by Erik Wesner, but Erik states some interesting observations about why the Amish tend to be successful through multiple generations. Here's what Erik shared;

The failure of Amish enterprises is less than 5% over a 5 year period as compared to a failure rate above 65% for comparable small-business start-ups across America.

The basic Amish business principles for SUCCESS are:

Integrity, family, and simplicity

There are two main Amish business concepts
- A. Business is a vehicle for something more important
- B. You can't do it all on your own

And best of all, Erik provided us what he believes are the secrets to their SUCCESS:

The 10 Amish Business SUCCESS Strategies:
1. The customer is always right—even when he's wrong.
2. The Golden Rule is always the rule.
3. The importance of quality goes without saying—protect it at all costs.
4. Word of mouth is the most powerful way to secure customers—it can be worth losing money to maintain a good reputation.

5. Know and understand the 80/20 Rule—focus your energies on the top 20% and miracles will happen.

6. At the same time—don't step on the small (small orders or small requests)...a trifling request sometimes is just a test run from someone that will end up in the top 20%.

7. Put aside your ego and listen to the customer—they will tell you what they want and how to sell it to them if you just take the time to listen.

8. Unhappy customers talk faster and louder than happy ones. Put the fires out quickly.

9. Handling difficult customers takes tact and you may have to lead destructive customers to the competition.

10. Being choosy is not a luxury available to all—predictive wizardry is as much art and intuition as it is science.

So there you go, I'm not Amish and you likely are not either, but we can certainly learn from brilliance no matter the source. The key here is...how will YOU utilize it?

"The only time to look down on someone is when you're bending over to help."
—Amish Proverb

Which one of the 10 Amish Success Strategies can I implement into my life or business immediately and how will I do it?

_____

_____

_____

_____

_____

_____

_____

_____

_____

_____

_____

_____

_____

_____

_____

_____

_____

PROVEN WAY #9
SUCCESSFUL PEOPLE HAVE A WINNING MINDSET

Typically, I don't watch a lot of regular television but I do have two exceptions for cutting the TV on in my office (now lovingly called the Bullpen).

I really love baseball, so 3 or 4 nights a week during baseball season; I pull out a book, sit in my massage chair and read with a baseball game on. Over the years, I've learned from and highlighted thoughts from hundreds of Masters and can still look up for a moment and cheer when something awesome happens in the game (isn't instant replay incredible!).

My other TV vice is the Olympic Games.

I have to admit that my brain gets a little fried from watching television over 17 days, but watching those incredible athletes and listening to their stories inspires me to push myself towards bigger goals and higher heights, and they always give me some great material for speeches and presentations.

Occasionally, a story sticks with me for years and one of those stories happened during the XXII Winter Olympic Games.

Leading the Canadian Women's Hockey Team 2 to 0 with less than 4 minutes in the third and final period, our American team seemed to retreat to a defensive mindset.

Rather than continuing to press hard with their powerful offensive surge, they chose to protect their lead, wait it out, and celebrate the Gold.

Canada saw it differently. Their coach went into scramble mode, removed the goalie from the net, added another offensive skater to the ice and attacked the American Women's Hockey team with all their skill, holding nothing back while using maximum effort for the last couple nail biting minutes.

Canada went ***ALL IN***, tied the game with 55 seconds on the clock and then won the contest in overtime. Canada wins the **GOLD***!*

After that incredible match and with both teams standing on their prospective steps of the podium, the Canadians smiled and cheered while the Americans cried and hung their heads.

One American athlete even chose to not accept her Silver Medal as it was presented.

Amazing! I felt so sorry for our young women.

The lesson was simple and profound…you have to play to *WIN* and not to *NOT LOSE*.

Life is just like that every day for you and for me.

Keep your head in the game, focus on your priorities, go ***ALL IN***, and play with a passion to win!

You might be disappointed and even a little frustrated if you end up with the silver, but when that happens, you'll also be motivated towards greater SUCCESS the next time.

The XXII Winter Olympic Games are just a memory now, but I don't think I'll ever forget the feeling I had when I watched that story transpire…just think how it would have felt if we were one of the athletes.

"You must accept that you might fail; then, if you do your best and still don't win, at least you can be satisfied that you've tried. If you don't accept failure as a possibility, you don't set high goals, you don't branch out, you don't try—you don't take the risk."

—*Rosalynn Carter*

How can I make sure I "GO ALL IN" today so I don't end up disappointed or frustrated with the results?

PROVEN WAY #10
DEEP KNOWLEDGE VS. DEEP SKILLS

You can know HOW to ride a unicycle, but you'll need deep skills to ride it backwards.

You can know HOW electricity works, but you'll need deep skills to rewire a skyscraper.

You can know HOW to swing a baseball bat, but you'll need deep skills to hit a 102 mile per hour fastball.

You can know HOW to play the trumpet, but you'll need deep skills if you plan to play *Flight of the Bumble Bee* in your senior recital.

So, the important question is...How often do you need both deep knowledge and deep skills?

A surgeon needs both deep knowledge and deep skills to save lives (and you get how important that is when YOU are on the table).

A pilot needs deep knowledge and deep skills when the computer goes out in the cockpit.

The answer lies in determining how often you expect people to choose YOU as their trusted advisor or their go to EXPERT.

Knowing HOW will get you paid, Deep Knowledge and Deep Skills will make you RICH.

When you're convinced that T.O.M.A. (Top of Mind Awareness) is important, or necessary, or critical to your SUCCESS, you'll have to move from just knowing HOW to develop Deep Knowledge and Deep Skills.

In today's world, all it takes to acquire deep knowledge and deep skills is time, desire and a willingness to not be lazy…no excuses…GO DO IT!

And here's your competition.

According to the Harvard Business Review, only 10% of the world's population has what's called "the learning mindset." The learning mindset people are those who seek out and enjoy learning. The other 90% will not look to improve their skills unless they have to as part of their job requirement.

Isn't that amazing!

There's an old saying that goes "An investment in knowledge pays the best dividend."

Even if you are not an NFL football fan, you likely know that a couple of years ago, the Denver Broncos got crushed by the Seattle Seahawks in the Superbowl.

On the Monday immediately following the big game, an ESPN analyst asked Peyton Manning, quarterback of the Denver Broncos and a shoo-in for the NFL Hall of Fame, a question that to some might have appeared ridiculous and insensitive (I'm one of the people that felt that way).

The question was; "Are you embarrassed by your team's performance?"

Ever the class act, Peyton simply replied……*"I would never use that word embarrassed. We did a lot right to get to this place."*

Peyton continued patiently and eloquently by saying......
.."We'll just need to choose to shake this off and get back to the skills that brought us here!"

At times, your life and mine are exactly like what happened that Sunday evening to the Denver Broncos. There are moments that just don't work out as we planned. In fact, we get crushed.

We have both a deep knowledge and deep skills and it still didn't happen for us that time.

Next time the worst happens for you, try following the wise Peyton Manning advice.

Choose to shake it off and get back to the skills that you know created SUCCESS for you in the first place.

And, you just might win YOUR Superbowl, because deep knowledge and deep skills will always play in your favor.

Knowledge without practice is useless. Practice without knowledge is dangerous!
—*Confucius*

What is the ONE SKILL you need right now that could help you more consistently produce at a higher level?

PROVEN WAY #11

9.5 ACTION STEPS TO IMPROVING YOUR LIFE

During the many years I've been a speaker and coach, I've received a number of calls, emails and cards from really good folks seeking systems and ideas to improve their circumstances.

There's rarely a quick and simple answer to their questions, so I've compiled a list of 9.5 things we can all do to make each and every year a little better.

1. Readers are Leaders, so there's really no excuse for you not reading at least one book every month no matter what your circumstances. The depth and ease of technology, digital books and audio recordings are right at your finger tips, so the only excuse for not reading is being lazy. Preferably read something that will grow your mind and make you think. I've heard it said that "a mind expanded with a new idea will never return to its original size."

2. Attend one or two programs, classes, or seminars every year that will help you improve your skills (church or those regular meetings you attend for work are not counted here). Make it something new that will stimulate a new normal for you and teach you new ideas and skills or at least help you implement some old ideas.

3. Read two or three blogs every week to help you gain a fresh perspective. They don't have to be long, so Mark's Minute would count too!

4. Invest 10 minutes every week learning something new on YouTube, or watch a TED Talk, or check out something new at Khan Academy (Lynda.com and VTC.com might also work for you).

5. Pay it forward by helping someone that needs a lift. People need you and you'll feel better and be better for serving.

6. Take a few moments each morning to be grateful for what you already have. Your feet should never be planted in the day until you've expressed gratitude for several things you are already blessed with. For me, the day begins with prayer, but no matter how you choose to express your gratitude, I can guarantee you that GOD or the Universe is listening.

7. Create something new. Take a few minutes to write in your journal, build or draw something with your hands, or grow something cool. Not sure where to start.........take a walk and you'll come up with an idea.

8. Reread your Goals and Priorities. If you haven't written them down yet, today is the right day to begin a draft.

9. Get healthier. Life slows down when you're physically or mentally deflated...you already know that.

9.5 Take some time to relax. A 20 minute nap in the middle of the afternoon is refreshing and there's plenty of science now that proves siestas are mentally and physically good for you.

I hope you're already doing all of these and please don't make excuses that you can't fit them in your schedule. I promise that you can, and if you add up all 9.5, you'll see that the combined minutes spread throughout your week will generate way more positive results than negative effects. They WILL be worth your time!

If you're not already doing all of them, just decide to take on one that you are weak at, make it a priority and a habit and before you know it, you'll experience miracles you never thought could actually happen to you!

"How much longer will you sit back and wait for your dreams to come true?

Set a course of ACTION that will insure your dreams become realities."

—Mark Given

Of the 9.5 ACTION steps, which one do you need the most improvement on? When will you begin?

PROVEN WAY #12
THE BEAUTY IN SIGNATURE STRENGTHS

"Signature Strengths" refer to the character strengths that are most essential to who YOU are.

Studies show that when we first see a person, we very quickly judge and categorize them (just 50 milliseconds) by how they look, what they wear, by their body language and by their facial expressions.

These are at best superficial indicators of their real values and competencies, yet we all judge none the less.

But underneath each of our professions, appearance, life role, or observable talents are what psychologists call "Signature Strengths"…or, who we truly are.

Signature Strengths **are not** about our professional talents and skills.

Signature Strengths **are** about the virtues and moral values we cherish.

At times, we see people struggling with their personal identity and how their personal feelings are at odds with the organization they serve.

You may sometimes feel miserable when you perform duties or practices that are opposite to your internal compass too.

Recently, while reading about and researching my own Signature Strengths, I found an interesting free survey that helped me identify my core values and ideals.

I thought you might be interested in seeing yours too?

If you're unhappy and don't know why, check out this link for a free evaluation.

www.viacharacter.org/www/Character-Strengths-Survey

The survey takes about 10 minutes, but the conclusions are interesting.

"Success is achieved through developing Signature Strengths, not by focusing your efforts on eliminating weakness."
—Mark Given

What would you consider is one of your Signature Strengths and how can you develop it further? When will you begin?

_____

_____

_____

_____

_____

_____

_____

_____

_____

_____

_____

_____

_____

_____

_____

_____

_____

*That's it.....that's all you accomplished?...
One Father's Day Card with Father of the Year in 1986?*

PROVEN WAY #13

13 POINTS TO CREATING YOUR SUCCESSFUL LIFE

Not long ago, I was fortunate to spend some time with Kevin Eastman and JP Clark. At that time, Kevin was Vice President of Basketball Operations for the Los Angeles Clippers (a brilliant leader and a deep thinker) and JP Clark was one of the Clipper Assistant Coaches (in my mind, JP is a rising NBA head coach).

We were all at an event learning from other Masters things we don't know that we don't know, and trying to hone our skills.

Kevin was invited to take the stage for about 45 minutes in a personal interview with the host, and he shared 13 great tips for building a life full of SUCCESS.

I wrote down each one and knew immediately that I would want to share them with YOU when I wrote this book. Here's what Kevin shared;

1. SUCCESS on a high level likely won't appear unless and until you're willing to get out of your comfort zone and change
2. SUCCESS is an exercise in inconvenience
3. SUCCESS only appears when we make a commitment to sacrifice
4. SUCCESS = A few simple acts continued day after day after day
5. SUCCESS is not created in a vacuum—it takes help
6. SUCCESS is found in simplicity rather than in sophistication

7. SUCCESS leaves footprints
8. SUCCESS finds solutions not blame
9. SUCCESS is a battle against fear
10. SUCCESS never comes through settling
11. SUCCESS has time zones—spare time vs. part time and full time vs. all the time
12. SUCCESS doesn't just network, it builds relationships
13. SUCCESSFUL people read, think, evaluate and then take ACTION

Kevin is a SUCCESSFUL man with a wonderfully SUCCESSFUL list.

I recommend you put his list to work in your life immediately!

> **"A successful man is one who can lay a firm foundation with the bricks others have thrown at him."**
> —*David Brinkley*

Of Kevin's 13 SUCCESS principles, which <u>one</u> could you implement <u>immediately</u> to help you move forward in your goals and dreams? When will you begin?

_____

_____

_____

_____

_____

_____

_____

_____

_____

_____

_____

_____

_____

_____

_____

_____

_____

PROVEN WAY #14
"JUST A LITTLE" MIGHT BE THE RIGHT AMOUNT

I keep observing that too generous amount of anything does more harm than good.

Just a little of that pecan pie is much better than the whole pie, because too much will make you fat.

Just a little bit of vacation is better than a lot of vacation, because too much vacation might make you lazy.

A good balance of money in your bank account is much better than winning that big lottery. Studies show that earning your living leads to better fiscal decision making and you'll appreciate what you have much more when you earn it.

A healthy amount of exercise every day is much better for you than a lot sporadically. Everyday exercise should keep your body toned up, while too much exercise on any single day could get you injured.

Focus controlled throughout your day nearly always guarantees some level of SUCCESS, but when focus is uncontrolled it likely drives the people around you crazy.

A small amount of onions are delicious, while a pile of onions causes people to stand way out of your personal zone.

Joy comes best in little pieces. If you felt joy every minute of every day, joy just wouldn't be as joyful.

Writing long detailed chapters full of stories, anecdotes and statistics might show some brilliance, but limiting it to brief Proven Ways keeps people reading and makes the point without wasting their time!

"We can all be just a little better. We can all try just a little harder."
—*Gordon B Hinckley*

Today is the best day to be a little better at _____?
How do I do it and exactly when will I begin?

PROVEN WAY #15
PRACTICE MAKES BETTER

Practice makes perfect…right?

Not really. Only perfect practice makes perfect.

If what you are doing is not working the way you thought it should be working, or the way the experts told you it would work for you, perhaps you're practicing incorrectly.

Maybe it's time to stop, re-evaluate and adjust?

You have to practice, practice, practice, but the practice won't help you get the results you desire unless you're focused on perfect practice. Just investing time in the 10,000 hour rule isn't good enough.

Some would argue in the baseball world, that Ted Williams is the greatest hitter to ever play the game.

But, Ted Williams took 1000 practice swings every day, about 900 more than anyone else of his day, and that is why hitting "*came easy*" to him. I'd wager that Ted's secret was not just in all those extra swings, but also in the extraordinary attention he placed on perfection.

The great martial arts Master Bruce Lee once said, *"I do not fear the man who has tried 10,000 kicks. I fear the man who has practiced one kick 10,000 times."*

This particular Proven Way may also relate to something in the archery world called the Archer's Paradox.

The physics of archery is more than just shooting an arrow at a target.

A Master Archer will account for the oscillation of the arrow during the release in order to consistently hit the sweet spot on the center of the target.

A Master Archer will evaluate and measure the quality of the tools and the current conditions of the wind and the weather.

Life is much like an Archer's Paradox.

When we won't take the time to consider what's actually happening (our current reality), or what's about to happen (our upcoming reality), a paradox sets in and distracts us from reaching our full potential.

In other words, we'll be off target.

Although ready, fire, aim works in some life and business circumstances…ready, aim, fire most often gives us the highest and best results.

When you take the time to practice, practice, practice, prepare, prepare, prepare and also provide yourself with the best tools for SUCCESS, you'll hit your bullseye much more consistently.

Show a little patience. Prepare a little more. Practice more than the average person thinks is necessary. That's when you deserve the BEST that life and work has to offer!

> **"Only those who have the patience to do simple things perfectly will acquire the skill to do difficult things easily."**
> *—Mark Given*

My life would improve if I focused more attention towards and better practice habits on _____?

What will I do and exactly when will I begin?

_____

_____

_____

_____

_____

_____

_____

_____

_____

_____

_____

_____

_____

_____

_____

_____

How much would it cost to just skip all the practice and go right to virtuoso?

PROVEN WAY # 16

BAD THINGS HAPPEN TO GOOD PEOPLE

We've all seen it…just watch the news.

Bad things happen to very good people.

But, when they're determined, good people overcome the bad things that happen to them.

How do they do it…with conscious effort, a lot of help and grit.

Recently, I wrote a new thought in my little pocket pad that goes like this…

"Through dedicated focus and forgiveness, weak things become strong." —*Mark Given*

It's only through conscious effort and a willingness to forgive do we overcome our significant challenges.

In a 2012 Huffington blog post, Linda Durnell wrote:

> "I believe each of us has an innate capacity for strength and throughout our lives, we develop — through conditions we find ourselves in — the skills to be secure, passionate, formidable and determined."

I agree, but unfortunately (or maybe fortunately), it's through our difficult challenges that we grow, so when bad things happen to you… grid up your loins and show some grit.

We can't always predict the brutal things that are heading our way, but none the less, you know they are coming.

And even if you've had more than your fair share, don't give up.

When you fight through that pain and find yourself full of experience, take the opportunity to share it.

Someone else will need to hear your story.

Someone else will want to know they can make it through.

Bad things have happened to you because bad things happen to good people.

Now…press forward. There are really good days ahead.

> **"Never regret…If it's good, it's wonderful…If it's bad, it's experience!"**
> *—Victoria Holt*

What was the last bad thing that happened to you and how did you make it through? Who helped you? Who do you know that you can help? How will you help them? When will you begin?

_____

_____

_____

_____

_____

_____

_____

_____

_____

_____

_____

_____

_____

_____

_____

_____

_____

_____

PROVEN WAY #17
SUCCESS LEAVES CLUES

I've spent my entire life watching and learning from all levels of SUCCESSFUL people and you likely have too.

They come in all shapes and sizes.

They come from diverse backgrounds and cultures.

They are skilled in a myriad of industries, professions and talents (and I'm not ignoring mothers and fathers).

But, there's one thing that is consistent in all these people regardless of where they came from and no matter their expertise.

SUCCESS always leaves clues!

What's been most interesting to me though is that SUCCESSFUL people, regardless of their history have a relatively short list of traits that are both important and copy-able.

And, I'll bet you'd like to know what those traits are?

I'll call them my R&D (what I call R&D is likely different than what you think though).

To me, R&D stands for Rip Off and Duplicate!

So, let's begin ripping…

#1–A clear vision of WHAT they want—expert after expert and book after book will recommend that you picture in your mind exactly what you want, then write it down (I whole heartedly agree with that principle). Some will suggest you tell others. But, no matter what your system, if you don't know where you want to be, you'll never find your way there. SUCCESSFUL people know exactly WHAT they want and WHAT they want to achieve. They can see exactly what it will look like, they can taste it, they can smell how the air will smell when they're there, and they can already feel the joy of knowing that they did it (think for a moment about all the stories you've heard about athletes that envisioned standing on that podium). SUCCESSFUL people don't get burdened with the HOW until they determine the WHAT.

#2–A focus that deters them from distractions—I've already talked about focus in Proven Way #6 (go back and read it again).

#3–A clear reality of "WHY" they are driven to make that specific thing happen—in the Amazon #1 Best Selling book that Don Greeson and I wrote together back in 2010 (Finding My Why, Ernie's Journey…A Tale for Seekers), you'll find reference to this exact principle. *"When your brain and your heart connect on the "WHY", the what and the how will appear."*

#4—A clear understanding that there is a difference between a Goal and a Priority.

Goals help you create actionable steps.

Priorities put the steps in order and WILL you towards the finish line.

5–A willingness to make mistakes and press on….nothing in life or business is ever permanently smooth, and when you're not making any mistakes, you're not taking any chances, so SUCCESSFUL people are willing to clean it up and press on after that big mistake.

6 -The wisdom to ASK for help—no-one SUCCESSFUL ever made it on their own. No-one you know or will ever know is that smart or that lucky. It takes help to SUCCEED at anything and

everything, even if that arrogant jerk you know says they did it without any help at all.

So, go get to work on those 6 steps...you're the beginning of what's holding you back!

> **"The only difference between you and someone you envy is that you settled for less."**
> —*Dr. Phil McGraw*

If I were to choose one thing that I wanted to achieve beginning right now, what would it be?

www.MarkGiven.com | 73

PROVEN WAY #18
SYSTEMS KEEP YOU FROM GOING INSANE

You've likely heard the phrase, "all's well that ends well."

It is often credited as originating from a 1605 William Shakespeare play of the same name, but a little research shows that it more than likely came from a John Heywood poem written in 1546.

Not long ago, as I was traveling home from a full day of speaking and coaching, I listened to several hours of automobile university.

One of the recordings included Darren Hardy, then the Publisher of Success Magazine, interviewing a SUCCESSFUL company owner.

The interview was focused on why his salespeople had such a stellar year when other companies and sales people were struggling to compete.

The answers were simplistic, but not simple…the owner concluded that focus, consistent productive activities and regular contact with key clients (that contact I now refer to as "flow") were the key to their SUCCESS in difficult times.

If that information was accurate, then we should consider a new phrase; "All's well that starts well"…

Ask yourself these questions:
1. Do I have successful systems in place to begin each day?

2. How do I begin and organize my week?
3. Should I consider making some changes in order to have a terrific year?
4. What are my plans to create a productive life outside of work so I can do a stellar job while at work?

4.5 Do I have the right people in place to help me succeed?

I stress a lot about focus and flow, and I'll keep doing just that. Likely, we all should, because to get a great start and keep things flowing, we need significant systems in place which will help us create a positive end.

And significant systems work in all facets of our life and business.

Athletes are taught that when simple activities are repeated over time, a long-term muscle memory is created for that task, eventually allowing those same muscles to perform efficiently without conscious effort.

A quality system with perfect practice can maximize our abilities which can lead to improved times and winning competitions.

So is muscle memory really about your muscles or is it actually about your brain utilizing a significant system?

Can that same concept be used to succeed in life and in business? I believe that it can.

Do you sometimes wonder why some people achieve more than you? If you do, then you likely have not invested enough time developing significant systems that for you would create muscle memory and guarantee success?

How much time and effort do you invest in researching and discovering systems that work? Are you reading, observing, studying, attending programs and classes then applying what the Masters do to become a Master yourself?

Powerful systems will lead to exceptional performance regardless of your area of interest. Decide what you want then go to work finding that significant system.

Several studies have shown that it takes 10,000 hours to become a Master at anything. I believe it, so go find that system and you can Master anything.

> **"A complex system that works is invariably found to have evolved from a simple system that works."**
> *—John Gaule*

What simple system could I implement today that would help me increase my numbers or improve my results right away? Where will I find it or what do I already have that I am not doing?

PROVEN WAY #19
WORKING ON VS. WORKING IN YOUR LIFE

There's a BIG difference between working ON your life and working IN your life.

Working ON your life moves you closer to the SUCCESS you are seeking. Working IN your life helps you check the box on the many daily activities and tasks you must complete.

The problem for most people is that they stay so busy spending all their time working IN their life that they ignore investing any amount of time working ON their life. For these people, nothing really changes and they often live exhausted and disappointed.

Get committed to scheduling time every day to work ON your life and things WILL change…I mean dramatically change.

Working ON your life is defined as anything you do that can improve YOUR circumstances. Reading this book or any other good material for that matter (something more than just a love novel) would be a good example. Exercising, participating in an educational program or class or convention, writing in your journal, writing that book you've always wanted to write, attending a social event to network (and not just drink), having a meal or playing golf or spending time with an important mentor, writing or reviewing your goals, meditating or praying, serving someone, reaching out personally to a friend, writing thank-you notes, making a call or stopping by to wish someone a happy birthday, anniversary or congratulations. These are all good examples of working ON your life.

Working IN your life would be a list of all the daily activities you must do to stay afloat. Things like going to work, bathing, eating, or taking your kids to school, practice or to that ball game. It can also include your driving or commuting time while listening to music, maintaining your home, cleaning, folding and ironing your wardrobe, shopping, sleeping and a hundred other items.

Working IN your life is that long list of items that somehow have to get done or your life is a mess and you live stressed out.

But with some thought and with some effort, you CAN find a little time spread throughout every day to work ON your life and the more time you find, the better your life will become.

It may only be 5 or 10 minutes spread thoughout your day, a little here and a little there, but YOU have to do it. The battlefield of life is filled with people that don't (or won't).

With some thought and planning, you can get both IN and ON done very easily every day. You CAN figure this out.

As an example of combining working ON and working IN (and with no intention of boasting), right this very minute and with the sun just coming up, I'm writing Proven Way #19 on the balcony of our cabin overlooking a beautiful blue ocean while my wonderful bride of 40 years is snoozing away. We're on a cruise ship sailing towards Mexico and combining a 40th wedding anniversary trip with several hours a day (for me at least) of writing so I can finish my 7th book.

It would be nice to sleep in, relax and be a little lazy, but that just doesn't work for me and it wouldn't work for you either if you understand this important principle.

Now don't judge my wife because she is sleeping right now. Her goals are different for this trip, she deserves the relaxation time and she is getting the things done she planned on this trip as well.

The point is, we're making a fun trip very productive while both working ON and IN our lives. If you aren't already, you should be doing it too....every day!

Now, you might say, Mark that works for you because you no longer have kids at home and your life is very different then mine.

I'm not at all sorry to say this, but that's just an excuse. Everybody can change and YOU can too! If your life is so full that you feel overwhelmed, it's time to take charge and find those brief moments throughout YOUR day to work ON your life. Skip ahead right now and read Proven Way #25, then come back.

Today, In this crazy world we live in, it might be a little strange to tell people that you love them when you don't really know them, but I need you to know that you are loved. I'm just one of the people that cares about you and just like all those people that do know you well, I'm rooting for you.

Don't be lazy. Don't make excuses. Go get what you deserve and YOU deserve all that life has to offer!

"The only place you find SUCCESS before work is in the dictionary."
—Mary V. Smith

Beginning today, what are the perfect times every day to commit to working ON my life?

PROVEN WAY #20
CHANGE YOUR MIND… CHANGE YOUR LIFE

A while back, I heard Dieter F. Uchtdorf say;

"Proper goal setting is NOT shooting an arrow at a blank wall, then drawing a circle around where it lands."

That's such an interesting way of describing how many people believe they have succeeded.

In reality, and most often, to change your life, you first must change your mind.

Big things happen when we clarify our beliefs.

Great things happen when we Master productive habits.

Amazing things happen when we create, then exercise positive behaviors.

Socrates is believed to have said something similar too;

"People are smart; they already have the answers within them."

I believe Socrates was correct in that thought.

In fact, you've seen it happen over and over in your life.

Someone asks you for your opinion of what they should do, but what they really want is just reinforcement of what they already know they should do.

They just need to hear you say it so they know they are right.

With all that said, let me repeat…if you want to change your life…change your mind.

And yet…maybe what I should say is…if you want to change your life, change your <u>actions</u>, but then I really can't make up my mind!

> **"You didn't get this way overnight, you're not going to change at the speed of light!"**
> —*Janice Given*

If I deeply want to Succeed, what is one thing I need to immediately change my mind about?

PROVEN WAY #21
SUCK IT UP!

My coach James Malinchak has repeated the following statements for years and they are just as relevant for you as they are for all his coaching clients;

"Don't just go through it, grow through it." and...

"Don't be a whiner, be a warrior."

Growth and improvement never come from worrying, whining or complaining.

It's hard to except that we're not at least a little alone when we're experiencing some pain though.

And yet, common sense would confirm that;

Sometimes, life is tough on you.

Sometimes, you don't get that break you think you deserve.

Sometimes, people don't treat you the way you know you should be treated.

Sometimes, your week is pressing you to a breaking point.

Sometimes, your house of cards is tumbling down all around you.

You already know that there are many things you cannot control, but you also know that there is one thing you can control…YOUR reaction.

So…What Are *You* Really Worried About?

You see the problem everywhere. There are so many folks that bite your head off for no good reason, or shoot you a not so

www.MarkGiven.com | 85

flattering gesture because they didn't get their way, or give you a glare that you wonder just how unhappy must their lives really be and how much pressure must they be under?

All this worry and stress can't be healthy!

Sometime back, The Nightingale Conant Company released a study on Stress and Worry.

Here's their authoritative estimate of what most people worry about:

Things that never happen = 40%–and yet people get totally stressed to the point of having a stroke because they fear it could.

Things over and past that cannot be changed by all the worry in the world—Nightingale Covenant discovered that 30% of the things people worry about have already happened and can no longer be changed.

Needless worries about our health—12% of people needlessly worry about their personal health although they realize they have no control over their family history or the circumstances that can often cause bad health.

Petty, miscellaneous worries of no consequence—10% add to their worries because someone convinced them that they should be worried.

Actual real, legitimate worries—only 8% of the time do you have a legitimate circumstance or situation that you should fear and worry about.

Please read that all again! Only 8% of your worries are actually worth concerning yourself about. 92% of your worries are pure fog with no substance at all and nothing you can do about them anyway.

Interesting and eye opening isn't it?

So, suck it up and get back to work...unless you're actually experiencing something in that 8%, and even then, you should suck it up and figure out what you can do about it.

Today IS the day to get back on track by not worrying about 92% of the things you can not do anything about.

And you've seen it happen over and over...when people suck it up, fight through their struggle and get back to it...a miracle is often just around the corner (or at a minimum a tender mercy).

YOU can consider that a guarantee!

> **"Let our advance worrying become advance thinking and planning"**
> *—Sir Winston Churchill*

Write a list of things you are currently worrying about and decide right now which ones you will release.

I'm worried that I don't have something to worry about!

PROVEN WAY #22
IT'S NOW HOW YOU WOW!

Amazon changed how we buy books and then almost everything else we buy.

Netflix and Redbox changed how we rent movies.

Airbnb has changed the short term stay.

Uber and Lyft have changed public transportation.

Yelp is changing the future of YOUR referral business.

And…there are hundreds of other great examples.

The status quo has changed and whether you are ready or not, it will continue to change.

Change may be hard, but YOU can change the status quo too.

I was listening to a Success Magazine interview a while back on my way to the airport, and Darren Hardy (the then Publisher of Success Magazine) shared a valuable lesson he called **6 Ways to Disrupt YOUR Business** and I'll add my own thoughts in (parenthesis).

1. Eliminate customer pain points—(figure out what drives them crazy and remove it from your product or service).
2. Reduce complexity—(simplify the process and make it easier for them).
3. Provide more value—(ask them what they want and then give it to them. I've often said that if you can't name five things you offer that your competition doesn't then you're a commodity and just like the competition… that goes for business and personal relationships)

4. Run towards what your competition is running away from (if your competition is afraid, they might be leaving a huge opening and opportunity for your Success).

5. Embrace technology changes (everyone needs a technology specialist just to try and stay in the now and have a fighting chance).

6. Always be transparent and have complete integrity (TRUST is the foundation of all relationships be it personal or business).

We can watch while innovators change the world, or we can get to work and be the conduit for the change our families and our clients need to see.

Forget thinking out of the box to create the future (unless you're Elon Musk or Apple) and become the deliverer of the NOW.

Its how you make people feel RIGHT NOW that will win your SUCCESS.

> **"Yesterday is a canceled check, tomorrow is a promissory note; only today is legal tender, only now is negotiable."**
> *—Cavett Robert*

What's one thing you could do today to solve a problem or wow your customers, your spouse, your partner, your family or your friend that would make you unforgettable?

___

___

___

___

___

___

___

___

___

___

___

___

___

___

___

___

___

___

PROVEN WAY #23
HOW'S YOUR FUNNY BONE

Think back and try to remember if you watched the Oscar broadcast on television in 2014?

If you can't remember it or you missed out because you didn't turn on the TV, avoided internet news immediately thereafter, or rarely mixed with folks that talked current events and gaffs, you were unaware that John Travolta mangled Idina Menzel's name in his introduction of her performance on the big Oscar stage that night in front of millions of people across the world.

At the time, Idina Menzel was a huge Broadway star, having wowed audiences as Elphaba in Wicked the musical and was catapulted to greater SUCCESS outside of the theatre world because of her beautiful voice and fabulous rendition of *Let It Go* in Disney's movie *Frozen*. I know you've heard the song (maybe even taken the opportunity to sing along with your kids).

Immediately after his Sunday night gaff, John was the brunt of late night show host jokes while Idina flourished in positive attention.

Here's what we all should have learned though.

We all goof. Sometimes it's more public than other times, but it's just part of life. When we fail or blunder, SUCCESS and opportunity can still appear through how we *choose to react*.

I heard some time ago that it takes three bones to SUCCEED in any circumstance...

A *Wishbone*—dream big, aim high, make a wish and be open to the possibilities that unfold.

A *Backbone*—SUCCEEDING and surviving take grit, guts, determination and perseverance.

And a *Funny Bone*—accepting and tickling that funny bone makes our life journey so much more palatable.

The cool thing about John Travolta was that he sucked it up, took all those cool invitations that came his way because of his mistake, found a really thick backbone and joined in the joke with his funny bone……..he maximized the joy in the ride while it lasted, shrugged it off and kept himself in a very positive light.

When things go bad, you can do that too…just find YOUR Funny Bone!

> **"It is of immense importance to laugh at ourselves. When we can begin to take our failures less seriously, we cease to be frozen by them!"**
> —*Mark Given*

What can I do to join in the fun next time I say something foolish? What can I do to tickle their funny bone rather than hide my face in embarrassment? (This is not an easy question, but is worthy of consideration)

PROVEN WAY #24
WHEN YOU NEED SOMETHING…ASK

If you know me well, have heard me speak or have been reading my weekly Mark's Minutes for a while, you know that Gigi (my lovely bride) and I have 5 grown children and currently have 6 grandchildren.

We've lived our entire adult lives trying faithfully to serve our family and provide a healthy and happy life for them.

And with that effort has come hundreds of requests for loving assistance from our gaggle of a family (I mean that in a humorous and good way).

So here's one of the many things I have learned…..If you want something, you have to ask for it!

Jack Canfield wrote about this very principle some years back and here are his 5 tips for getting started on receiving what you want;

1. Ask as though you actually expect to get it.
2. Assume you can actually receive it–don't start with an assumption that you can't get what you want.
3. Ask someone who can give it to you–or at least someone who can help you get it.
4. Be specific about what you want–vague requests produce vague results.
5. Ask repeatedly but not obnoxiously–persistence is a key principle to SUCCESS.

I love the clarity of Jack's simple process and it really works.

Decide what you want, then ask for it…simple.

It seems like a lifetime ago, but on many weekends for many years, our family traveled together and performed as a family band under the name of Boys Club and a Babe (you can look us up and find us on YouTube). The Given children Blaine, Chase, Kyle, Taylor and Kerrilyn were the featured performers and Janice and I were there for support, direction and protection.

We have a thousand inside stories of funny things that happened over those nearly 20 years and all the strange people we met.

Some, we'll never forget. Here's just one of the stories:

On an unusually warm night, sometime in the very early 2000's, an unusual looking and very inebriated woman dancing directly in front of the stage while attending a North Carolina street festival shouted a classic line to one of our kids never by us to be forgotten…she said;

"Be careful what you ask for…you might just get it!"

Our dancer was of course referring to herself (which made the line even more amazing and humorous), and that remark has been repeated in our family hundreds of times since that night.

But here's the more amazing thing…she was right!

She still is right.

It's when you fail to ask that you likely fail.

When you really need something, gather up the gumption to ask. When your gut tells you the time is right and the person is right and the need is right, follow that prompting and ask.

And never forget…

Be careful what you ask for…you might just get it!

(And just in case you're wondering…our son did NOT take her up on her offer!!)

> **"If there is something to gain and nothing to lose by asking, by all means ask."**
> *—W. Clement Stone*

Is there something I should be asking for right now? What is it, who should I ask and when exactly will I ask?

PROVEN WAY #25
4 STEPS TO SUCCEEDING AT ANYTHING

I've been blessed to speak, teach or present at more than a thousand events the past two decades and have met tens of thousands of wonderful people trying their hardest to create a life of significance.

It would be a reasonable wager to say that each of them were seeking the same thing.

SUCCESS!

Although defined differently by many of them, they were none the less seeking their version of the same need…to feel like their life has added some value to the people they love, to have given their best at their chosen industry or profession and in some way, made the world a little better because they lived.

So…if you feel the same (and I bet you do), here is some of the magic you are seeking to fulfill your need.

1. **Decide What YOU Want**—Be specific. Most people struggle because they cannot decide. <u>What do you really want?</u> How much money do you want to make and how much money do you want in your bank account? What do you want to have and achieve in your life? Are you seeking a simple life or one of influence? <u>What do YOU want to BE?</u> What do you want to do with your life while you are living and what do you want to be remembered for when you're gone? Do you want to be famous or will you be satisfied just being famous in your family circle or group of friends?

<u>Where do YOU want to go?</u> Where do you want to live, in what kind of home? Do you want to travel…then where? What do you want to see and experience?

2. **Create YOUR Plan**—It's only after you are specific about what you want and then follow it up by writing it down can you create YOUR winning plan. The truth is, this is just one book in thousands of self-help books that share strategies for SUCCESS, but you have to search in your heart for what will work for YOU. YOU have to determine some plan and then commit to put in the effort which will make your plan work. You can find hundreds of Master Systems that claim they work, but the million dollar question is…will it work for YOU? You'll never know unless you complete #1 and then put pencil to paper and write your own #2. Study as many as you can find, then create a plan that fits YOU. Your need…Your want…Your SUCCESS.

3. **Estimate the Cost**—There is always a cost. It may be in money. It will definitely be in time. Likely, it will be both and every time you say yes to one thing, you're saying no to something else. Before you begin YOUR work towards SUCCESS…do the math. The math never lies. In my experience as both a seeker and a coach, whatever you think it will cost…time or money or both…double it and maybe triple it! If you discover you're not willing to pay the cost, go back to #1 and #2 and start again, because you'll never SUCCEED if you're not willing to pay #3!

4. **Don't Let Anyone Take it From You**—The world is full of naysayers. Many of them are your family and your friends. They mean well. They'll call themselves devil's advocates. They don't want you to experience pain. They're challenged by YOU being challenged. They say they only want the best for

YOU, but it's all a bunch of horse manure! If YOU are really committed to #1 and #2 and #3 then don't let <u>anyone</u> steal your dream. You can do it! There is very little in this world that is not achievable when you are truly committed to making it happen. So get to work! Change YOUR life! YOU deserve all of it!!

> **"For true SUCCESS, ask yourself these four questions: Why? Why not? Why not me? Why not now?"**
> — *James Allen*

#1—Decide what YOU want?

_____

_____

_____

_____

#2—What's YOUR a plan (you'll likely need more paper)

_____

_____

_____

_____

#3—Estimate the cost?

_____

_____

_____

_____

#4—Who are the people that will try and talk me out of it?

_____

_____

_____

_____

ONE LAST MESSAGE FROM MARK

Thank-you!

A very dear friend of mine once said, *"If your dreams aren't big enough to make some people laugh out loud, they're just not big enough"* and I have witnessed that to be true over and over in my life.

I've learned through personal experience, through watching the lives of my own family and witnessing hundreds of people that I have mentored or coached that my friend was and is exactly right. Decide what you want and get to work making it happen. If it's a righteous desire that benefits others and you're willing to do the work, you can't stop it from happening. Now, of course it has to be reasonable, but why not dream big…really big.

Trust in the process.

Why?

Because, when you do…God and the Universe will conspire to make it happen.

So, thank-you for taking your valuable time to invest in you by reading this book…but reading is just the first step.

Now you have to go out and actually apply it every day of your life.

You can do it and the time to start is right now!

I'm hoping you know that I'm just one of the people rooting for your success, so go get a piece of paper now and write down where and how you're going to begin building more success and added Trust.

Then, when it's convenient, drop me a note and let me know how it all worked out for you.......your SUCCESS story. I always love hearing SUCCESS stories and with your permission, it might just make my next book!

You can reach me at:
Mark Given International
P.O. Box 1460
Roanoke Rapids, NC 27870
mark@markgiven.com

You might also consider making the world a little better by sharing this book with someone else. If you choose to not give it away, please know that you can purchase as many extra copies as you want or need!

TRUST BASED
PHILOSOPHY

Written By Mark Given
Amazon #1 Best Selling Author, Southern Gentleman, Husband, Father, Grandfather, Relationship Expert, Sales Guru

mark@markgiven.com   www.markgiven.com

BONUS SECTION

BOOK BONUS

10 **MORE** WELL KNOWN SECRETS OF SOUTHERN HOSPITALITY

#1—Always speak a kind word

In the South, it's always the right time to say a kind word. In fact, it's expected. And a kind word is said in many different ways. Drive down the road just a piece and you'll know someone you're passing is also from the South because they'll give you a nod, throw up a hand or maybe a finger signifying their kind how do you do (that's howdy in the South and the finger they show won't be the same finger they seem often to throw up in the North).

#2—Treat everybody generously

In the South, you wouldn't dare invite someone in to your home and not show them a place to sit and then offer a beverage. My wife will remind me in a minute of the time she and her dear mother Mom El stopped by to visit a member of the church and the woman let them stand in the living room for 30 minutes, never inviting them to sit down or ask them if they'd like a drink (just makes you never want to go back, doesn't it).

If you pass someone that's struggling along the way, a multi generational Southern Gentleman or Southern Bell will reach out a hand offer some help. Maybe buy them a sandwich or give them a ride.

So, if you want to show true Southern Hospitality, when someone knocks at the door and you answer, invite them in, ask them to sit a spell and bring them a cold beverage.

When you find someone in need, help them. And you don't have to be rich to help, cause' we live by the parable of the widow's mite.

#3—Guests <u>is</u> the same as family

Some places across the US, people treat guests better than family, but in the South we treat them just as good as family. We'll feed them on our finest china and we'll invite them to sing along. We'll let them borrow our car or our trailer and take them fishin' just like if they were our uncle or our cousin.

#4—The handwritten word really matters

Emailing is fine and texting is simple. Facebook is convenient and a phone call is generous, but noting is as valuable and heartwarming as a hand written note, card or letter. People know you're important to them when you take the time to hand write a message.

Maybe it's because everybody knows it took a lot of time to hand write that first bible and it took some thought for your grandmother to write your grandfather.

Just put pen to paper and watch how people respond!

#5—Everybody's got a signature dish

In the South, everybody's got at least one signature dish and we can tell how good of cook you are by your <u>signin'</u>. Mine is grits. Gigi's is chicken pastry (that's chicken n' dumplins to some folks). My daughter in law Janelle's is tater tot casserole.

If you want to please a Southerner when <u>yer'</u> over for dinner and they ask what you'd like to eat, always ask for their signature dish, then don't forget to compliment them on it after you finish lickin' the plate.

If you want to get invited back, send them a handwritten note afterward to tell them how delicious it was. They'll love you forever!

#6—Traditions is important
Just like many cultures, Southern families have traditions.

You can always tell a Southerner 'cause they pull over when a funeral is passing by. We take food to people in times of sadness. We still go to church. We like to sit on the front porch and sip a cold beverage. We still like to go visit family, especially the older folks and in our smaller towns, we still have an ice cream truck that stops by so we can buy a treat for the young varments. The South is a great place to live. If you've never tried it, just come for a long visit.

#7—It's tough to beat anything that was canned
Canning is not really in a can in the South. Cannin' works best in jars. Pickles, maters, figs, sweet potatoes, butter beans, sweet corn...just cook em' up and drop em' in a Mason Jar. Stack em' deep on the shelf and you're prepared for winter. If you do it right and your garden was productive, you jarred more than enough so you could give some away. Now that's a Southern gift you can sink your teeth in.

#8—If you leave hungry, it's your own fault
Spend a little time in the South and you'll discover that we love to eat and we know how to lay out a spread that's both mouth watering and belly filling. Just look at our people. Skinny Southerner is actually an oxymoron. Who wants to be one of those! So come on down and join in the festivities. We eat three hardy meals a day, so if you leave hungry, it's your own fault!

#9—Religion is our way of life
In the South, we got thousands of churches and dozens of religious beliefs. Southern Baptist churches have lots and lots of versions and may have the biggest congregations, but we don't leave out

the Methodists, Lutherans, Pentecostals, Episcopalians, Catholics, Seventh Day Adventists, Jehovah Witnesses or the Mormons. And that's not all of them, there's a whole lot more. Drop by any older Southern town and you'll find 2 or 3 churches on any particular corner spread all across the community (cities build drug stores and convenience stores that way in the North).

And...if you want an inside secret, keep an eye on local announcements for upcoming Homecomings...

Just drop by. The food will be outstanding, I guarantee they'll be glad to see ya' and you can just about bet that they'll invite ya' back!

#10—Yes Mam' and No Sir ain't just for Ma and Pa

As a Southern Pa and Grand Pa, it's becoming more difficult to get Southern kids to ALWAYS say yes Mam' and yes Sir, no Mam' and no Sir, but the tradition is as important as remembering that Richmond was the Capital of the Confederacy.

The Civil War is a fact of history, the South was wrong about slavery, and the Lord continues hard to balance it all out, but some things just ain't worth changin'. One of them is showing respect.

So, in my mind, no matter how many Northerners move to the South, there's no excuse for letting the kids off the hook.

Your Ma and your Pa deserve respect and there should be no argument ever about how we treat our Grandma and Grandpa and if you're lucky, your Great Grandma or your Great Grandpa.

I can't speak for the North, but in the South, yes Mam' and yes Sir and no Mam' and no Sir should be as natural as cotton in the field and breathin'!

ADDITIONAL BOOK BONUS

MARK GIVEN INTERVIEWED BY JACK CANFIELD

Jack Canfield: Hi. I'm Jack Canfield, co-author of the New York Times number one best-selling series, *Chicken Soup for the Soul*, co-author of *The Success Principles*, and a featured teacher in the movie, *The Secret*. I'm sitting here today in an interview with Mark Given. I find Mark to be one of the more interesting and fun people I've ever interacted with, so I'm looking forward to our interview today.

Mark Given: Thank you.

Jack Canfield: Let's start with this, just tell our viewers a little bit about who you are and what you do.

Mark Given: Well, Jack, I've spent nearly 40 years studying the science and the art of building trust.

I've written several books on this important subject, directed towards trust based leadership, trust based selling, and trust based success. I travel the country doing mostly keynotes and breakout sessions, half day, or full day sessions, sometimes multi-day sessions on teaching the four steps, or the four stages of trust to companies, and organizations, and associations, and groups that want to succeed by understanding the importance of building trust with their customers and clients, or with their staff, with their employees, with all the people they serve, even their own families.

It's fun. It's exciting. It's interesting to see people when the lights come on and they realize that trust is the foundation of everything. When people lose trust, it's difficult to rebound.

It is so very important that we teach these four stages of trust that are critical to success and are relevant to what all of us do.

Jack Canfield: I'm going to ask you about those four stages in a moment.

Mark Given: Good.

Jack Canfield: But, before I do that. I know you're very passionate about what you do. How did you get into trust being your focus? Why are you so passionate about it?

Mark Given: Well, Jack, there are probably a lot of reasons for that. First of all, when I graduated from college, all I really wanted to do was be in business. So, I went into retail for 20 years and had a pretty successful company in North Carolina, and Virginia. What I discovered was that if my employees didn't trust me, they would steal from me. If customers didn't like us and trust us, they would just do business with somebody else. I eventually sold that company and got into real estate. I discovered it was exactly the same thing with my customers, and clients, and all of the other people I worked with within the real estate industry.

When there's no trust, it's very difficult to succeed.

On top of all that and probably the most important thing personally is that my lovely bride of 40 years and I have five children, and we meant to do that.

I've discovered in life that maintaining trust with your spouse and with your children is critical to happiness and success. It's tough to be successful in any portion of your life when there's no foundation of trust.

I started studying that years ago, not realizing that I was studying the art and the science of trust, but I began by reading books. Books like yours Jack, *Chicken Soup for the Soul*. Many of the stories you included talk about trust, and love, and care and how people feel.

The Success Principles has many of the same principles. There are many other good, really powerful books, that in theory cover the art of building trust.

But I've also discovered that there are no tricks to it. It's just a simple, yet not simplistic science and an art to understanding how to be trustworthy. How you can show people that they can really count on you and care about you and that you care about them.

It's been exciting to spend all these years really studying the art and science of trust and developing some clarity on the 4 Stages of Trust.

Jack Canfield: You know it's funny. I hadn't thought of this in years, but I'm a human potential trainer.

Mark Given: Yes, of course you are.

Jack Canfield: I do workshops and so on. One of the first workshops I ever took was with a guy named Jack Gibb who wrote a book called Trust. He taught this model called TORI. Trust, T-O-R-I, trust leads to openness, openness leads to self-realization and realization of others, and that leads to interdependence and independence instead of co-dependence and dominate dependence.

Mark Given: Sure. That's correct.

Jack Canfield: That's so cool. Thank you for reminding me of one of the major pillars of my own consciousness.

Mark Given: That's terrific. I'm glad I could help just a little.

Jack Canfield: We talked about the 4 Stages of Trust. Talk about that a little bit.

Mark Given: Well, what we've discovered in our own studies is there is nothing else out there similar to what we've done, to individualize these 4 Stages of Trust.

But, there really are 4 stages.

The first stage is *The Introduction Stage*, or what I call, the **Grand Opening**.

There are several studies by highly respected Universities now that show people make a decision about you and me in 38 to 55 milliseconds. We've formed the same opinions just as other people form an opinion of us. We decide and they decide whether they like us or can trust us in less than a blink of the eye.

They decide whether they want to associate with us, or do business with us. They decide whether they want to be around us or not be around us that quickly.

And, the Grand Opening is just the 1st critical stage of trust.

The million dollar question then is; *how do we perform at a high enough level so we always have our best Grand Opening ready to deliver to everyone we meet…anytime…anywhere*?

The 2nd Stage of Trust is also very important. We call that the ***Rapport Building Stage***.

Stage 2 is where we get to know people. It's really more about learning to ask good questions and then really listening for the answers. There's an old Chinese proverb that says, "Listen with the intent to hear."

What I've discovered is that when we spend more time asking and then really listening, we become a friend and a confidant.

It is amazing how much we can learn about people and how you build a foundation of trust by just listening and not talking.

Jack Canfield: My wife always says to me, "You want to focus on being more inter-rested than being interesting."

Mark Given: That's right.

Jack Canfield: Exactly.

Mark Given: You go a lot further by being interested.

Jack Canfield: Exactly.

Mark Given: Then, the 3rd Stage of Trust is the ***Maintenance Stage***.

That's where we do all the things that are important to maintain trust. We do that by serving and being more of a giver than a taker.

We all know people that are givers. They are the kind of people we want to associate with.

The 3rd stage is all the skills necessary to become more giving.

Bob Burg and John David Mann wrote a wonderful book that reflects this stage perfectly.

It's called *The Go-Giver*. A very simple, yet powerful book.

Jack Canfield: I know, I've read that.

Mark Given: But this principle is also really profound. I've gotten to know both Bob and John for that reason. It's such an important book. It's being a giver instead of a taker. The world is full of takers.

Then, the 4th Stage of Trust is the one that we all need because sometimes we mess up, no matter how good we are, how smart we are.

It's the **Apology Stage** or what I also call the **Repair Stage**.

This stage is the science and the study of how to apologize. How do you repair the damage once you've made a mistake?

That really relates to companies as well as people. I mean, gosh, how many articles are there every day now, online about some company or individual that has damaged trust with their customers or associates, or the country or the world. It relates to business. It relates to life and it relates to our own personal relationships with the people we care about.

Those are the four important stages, and they're very separate because the skills necessary for each are very different. That's why I spend the time teaching people and speaking to people about how to be their best in each of the four stages.

Jack Canfield: Now I wish I had three hours, I'd literally attack all four of those in-depth. But, I will ask you one follow-up question. You talked about the 1st Stage and the **Grand Opening**, and you only have 55 milliseconds. That's 55 thousandths of a second.

Mark Given: That's right.

Jack Canfield: Which is like, how do you even measure that? But, give us a clue about how you, in that 55 thousandths of a second, what can, or should, someone do?

Mark Given: Well, of course it begins with the way you look. It's your facial expressions. It's the way you dress. Those are the simple things, the obvious things.

But I've discovered a more complex process. It's what we do in our verbal opening.

We've all been taught a standard opening or greeting. We call that a two-step greeting. It's goes……Hi, I'm ……

That introduction is focused on ourselves. It's all about ME.

What I've learned in all these years of research is that when we teach people to go from a two-step greeting to a three-step greeting that it changes the way people feel about us. And the bonus is that we actually listen better. It actually subliminally demonstrates interest in the other person.

As simple as that may sound, it's not simplistic. When we're teaching the **Grand Opening**, we spend some time teaching people to go from a two-step greeting to a three-step greeting, which opens up a whole new realm of trust. And the magic is that we do it in just the very first few seconds of meeting someone new.

It can also be used with people we already know well. As is said in some circles, the 3 Step Opening is a game changer.

Jack Canfield: What are those three-steps?

Mark Given: The three-steps are simple. You go from, it's all about me to it's really about you. And I mean that literally.

In other words, instead of saying, "Hi, I'm me." You would say, "Hi, it's good to see YOU (or something similar). I appreciate the opportunity for us to be here, Jack. Thank YOU for doing this. Then, I'd share my name."

We would actually use the word, YOU twice, instead of making it quickly about yourself.

Jack Canfield: Yeah, I hear that.

Mark Given: Instead of hey, or hi, or hello, I'm me. It's hello. It's good to see YOU. Thank YOU for interviewing me. Boy, sure appreciate YOUR time today.

When I get done with the three-steps, or the initial two-steps, then I get to the "I'm Mark Given."

But, what we've also found as a bonus is that when people go from a two-step greeting to a three-step greeting, they more often walk away and actually remember the name of the person that they just were introduced to.

Jack Canfield: Interesting.

Mark Given: Often, when you use the two-step greeting, you walk away and you forget. Now, what was her name again? We take memory courses and try to do all these things, and just going from a two-step greeting to a three-step greeting is a remarkable change in the science of trust, building trust and creating an immediate likeable bound.

Jack Canfield: That's fascinating. I'd love to interview you about all this. I'll have to take your course! And I can tell that you are passionate about this.

Mark Given: I am.

Jack Canfield: You've talked about why you're so passionate about it. There are a lot of people talking about trust. I know Stephen M.R. Covey and others. What makes your work different?

Mark Given: Well, what we've learned is there's really not a single person, there's not a company, or an association, or organization out there that has not benefited from our programs and teaching

	steps. Instead of just a concept of building trust, we actually teach people how to do it.
Jack Canfield:	How to do it and it is needed.
Mark Given:	And we teach the steps on how to do it. We do it in those different formats, in a keynote, or breakout, or a half for full-day session, so that we can actually delve into those 4 different Stages of Trust and teach them the techniques. There are a lot of motivational speakers out there, and certainly, we motivate, but the difference, I feel, and what makes me so passionate about this is, when I'm out speaking and I see the lights come on in their brain and they think, "Oh, I could use that. How did I not know that, or how did I miss that, or gosh, I just made that mistake, or I said something or I did something and here's how I fix it."
	It's really exciting to get those emails, or a note, or something from somebody that says, "Thanks for teaching me that. Thanks for helping. Here's what happened as a result. I went home and did this, or I had a customer or client, my best client, that I really messed it up and I've been able to repair that because of these important techniques."
	It's exciting to get up in the morning and get out and do what I do, because this changes lives. It changes businesses.
Jack Canfield:	You know, it's so sad that our schools don't teach these skills.

Mark Given: Sure. I agree.

Jack Canfield: I always tell people, "Tell me the five causes of the civil war." No one can even remember them, but we study that for days, or weeks. But, we're not learning communication skills, relationship skills, self-management skills.

It's like we have to go into the hotels and the conference centers to learn what's really important. You're out there doing that. That's great. When you look at the clients you have, are there common challenges that people are facing out there in relation to this? How do you help them address those?

Mark Given: Yes, Jack. What I've found is that we all make mistakes. We all want the same thing and that's to build trust with people. People that we care about, or people we want to associate with, or people we want to do business with.

The real challenge is that we all experience much of the same thing. We have good days and we have bad days. When we have those bad days, we need some methods to improve and to repair. Just look at the statistics on marriages these days and you can see that clearly, there's a need for what I do and have studied. Although, I spend the majority of my time in the business world, the relationship world, marital world, could also use the techniques and skills too.

It's really exciting and fun to get out and help people see that they can do it. It's not about

	what I've learned, or sharing some things, it's what they can actually go and apply immediately themselves.
Jack Canfield:	I'm sure you find too, like from my work, if I do a corporate training, the people take those same skills home with their wife, with their neighbors, in their church, with their children.
Mark Given:	Sure, absolutely.
Jack Canfield:	Absolutely, very good. If someone's sitting out there watching this, they're probably thinking, "Yeah, I don't know all that stuff about phases of trust and how to do it and I've lost some business because of, perhaps, betraying a trust, or not knowing how to build that rapport and trust." They're thinking about, perhaps, hiring you to work with them. What would you tell them?
Mark Given:	I'd say, "Please, give me a call."
Jack Canfield:	Plain and simple.
Mark Given:	Please give me a call, because I'm pretty confident that there's something, whether you're a leader and trying to build trust with your organization, your staff, or your employees, or whether you're a sales person trying to build trust with your clients or customers, or you're just trying to build a successful life.
	What I would say is that we have some things that can help you. That, given even just a little bit of time, we can share important

trust building systems that people can apply immediately. So they can go home or back to work and actually do something.

What's fun is to see people actually go home and do something. So, call me, they can reach me at MarkGiven.com. It's really easy to find me and I invite anyone that could benefit to do that.

Jack Canfield: You're not in the witness protection program.

Mark Given: I'm not, thank goodness, you can find me.

Jack Canfield: Very good, very good. Well, Mark, this is fascinating. I think trust is critical ... It's a foundational thing, that everything else is built on. If you don't have it, nothing moves forward. Thanks for being my guest today. I really appreciate it.

Mark Given: My pleasure Jack, absolutely my pleasure.

Jack Canfield: If you want to build more trust in your relationships, in your organization, if you want to teach your people, whether they're sales people, managers, whatever it might be, at your association meeting, or convention, your conference, an in-house workshop, whatever, Mark Given can help you do that. Check out his website at MarkGiven.com.

MOTIVATE AND INSPIRE OTHERS!

"Share This Book"

Retail $24.95

Special Quantity Discounts

5-20 Books	$21.95
21-99 Books	$18.95
100-499 Books	$15.95
500-999 Books	$10.95
1,000+ Books	$8.95

**To Place an Order Contact:
(252) 536-1169
www.MarkGiven.com**

THE IDEAL PROFESSIONAL SPEAKER FOR YOUR NEXT EVENT!

Any organization that wants to develop their people to become "extraordinary," needs to hire Mark for a keynote and/or workshop training!

"If you are looking for a speaker, trainer and coach that can empower, inspire, and motivate your group, then you must book my friend Mark Given!"

—**James Malinchak,** Featured on ABC's "Secret Millionaire" Best Selling Author of 20 Books

"We hire Mark to share his Trust Based Philosophy in leadership, sales and success with our 1500 members every year!"

—**Zan Monroe,** CEO Long Leaf Pine Association, Author, Speaker and Coach

"You are simply an event planners dream! I have been involved with contracting hundred's of speakers for various programs over the last 24+ years and I consider an exemplary example of an ideal speaker."

—**Rebecca Fletcher,** Director, GIRE, VP of Education

To Contact or Book Mark to Speak:
(252) 536-1169
www.MarkGiven.com